HAMBURGER HARRIET WON'T SETTLE

© 2024 AnnA Gomez

Published by ALPS, an imprint of Paraklesis Press

Interior design by: Sally Apokedak and Abigail Gabriel

Illustrated by: Abigail Gabriel

Cover design and art: Abigail Gabriel

Distributed by Paraklesis Press 2024

ISBN: 978-1-947446-32-8

In memory of my beloved
mother, Julia Breijo Muñiz, who led by
example and taught me to never settle. ~AnnA

This book belongs to:

_____

Once upon a time, there lived
a plain hamburger named Hamburger Harriet.

BURGER
BOULEVARD

Hamburger Harriet had lots and lots of brothers and sisters and dozens upon dozens of cousins.

There were so
many, she couldn't
tell them apart
because everyone
looked the same.
Same **boring,
brown meat.** Same
plain, boring bun.

Now Harriet's life as a burger was going well enough—she got to go to plenty of backyard barbecues,

she went on some great picnics,

and she was invited to all the children's birthday parties. Yet, deep down, she just wasn't satisfied.

Hamburger Harriet felt she was meant for something bigger and better than being just a **brown** burger in a **tan** bun.

"Where's the **JAZZ?**"
"Where's the **PIZZAZZ?**"
"Where's the tantalizing taste
that will *tickle* my tastebuds?"

These were the
questions Harriet would ask.

But none of her relatives could answer
because they were, after all, just a bunch
of boring burgers. Pitiful patties, one and all.

POP!

Hamburger Harriet wanted to cook up a change. She just couldn't take another day of **plain, round, and brown**. She was sure she could be a better burger. She knew she needed COLOR,

she knew
she needed
flavor,

and she knew
she needed ...
CRUNCH!

But nothing
she tried worked.

She decided to take
a long walk to clear her head.

Harriet was trudging down Burger Boulevard,
off Pickle Plain Lane, muttering to herself. Where, oh,
where could she find **COLOR** and *flavor* and **CRUNCH?**

And that's when she looked across the street and spotted …

...BLT Betty! The sun broke through the clouds on that no-fun Sunday and ...

FRESH LETTUCE

. . . HOLD THE KETCHUP!
An idea popped into Harriet's head. An idea for a
flavor mashup that would be as big as peanut butter and jelly.

Harriet could start a
partnership with
BLT Betty.

This could be a combo made for a toasted bun!

No longer
would Hamburger Harriet
be a boring burger, just plain and brown.

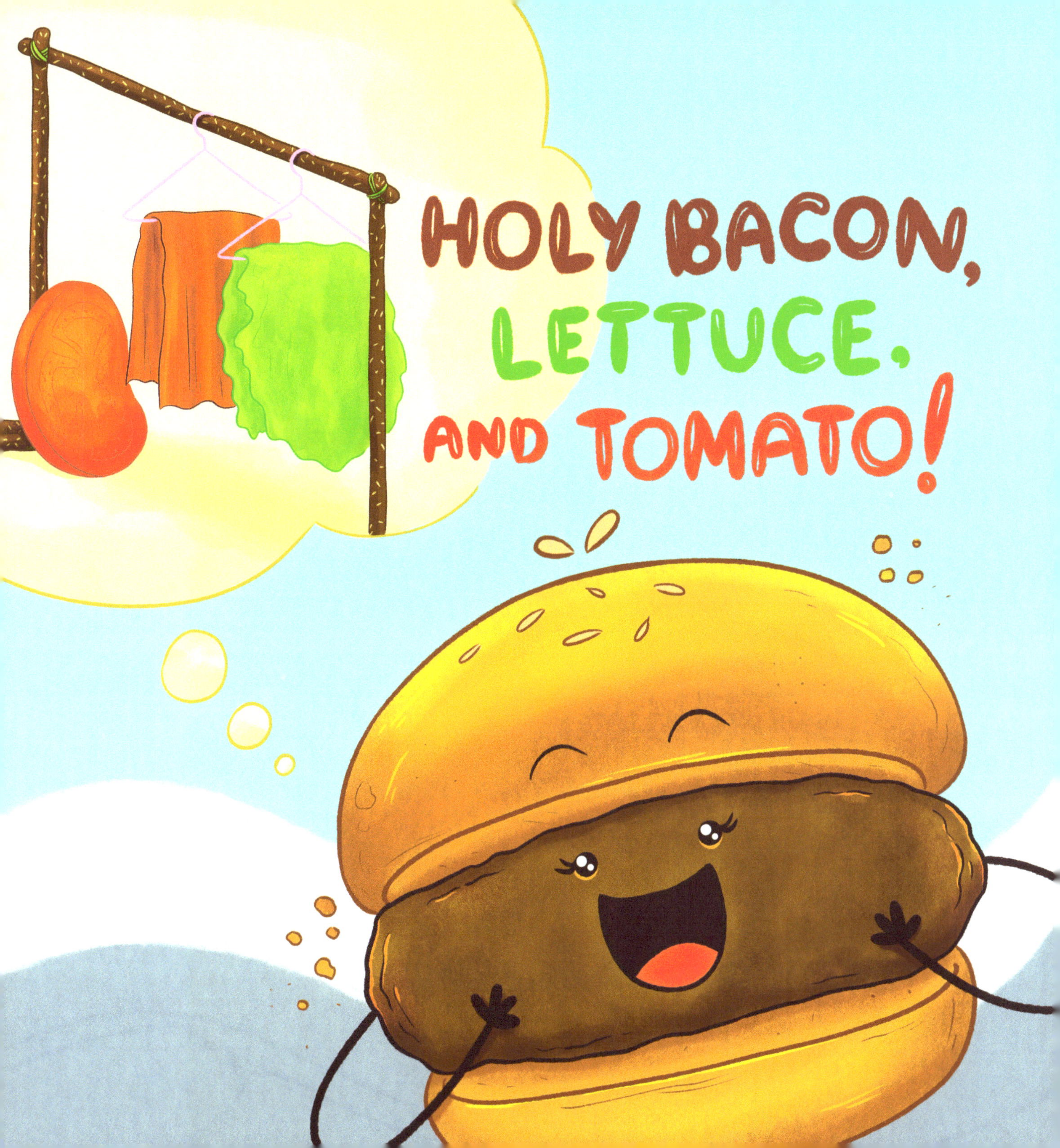

HOLY BACON,
LETTUCE,
AND TOMATO!

Hamburger Harriet
would finally be able to let her

inner glow

show with layers and layers of **flavors**.

"A **boring burger** no more!" she shouted. "I can finally be the burger I always wanted to be!" Harriet was so excited she was in danger of becoming bunless. All that was left to do was some convincing . . .

BREAD FOR YOU

So Hamburger
Harriet raced over
and had a chat with BLT Betty.

She explained what a delicious collaboration
their pairing could be, and she ended by saying,
"Betty … protein and color, sustainable and sweet …

… together we'll make the tastiest treat!"

Now BLT Betty was no silly sandwich, so she readily agreed. "Harriet," she exclaimed, "if I come with juicy toppings, and you bring your beef and bun, we'll make a great new sandwich with **COLOR**, *taste*, and **FUN!**"

LET'S

"LET'S DO IT!" they both shouted.
Really, who wouldn't want to be part
of the biggest burger breakthrough in history?

DO IT!

And so, the Bacon Burger Deluxe was born, and all adored it ... especially Harriet.

THE NEWEST
„SAVORY‿CRAZE‟
IN TOWN!

Let's think ...
Are you okay with your writing being **plain?**

YAAAWN...

What can help add **flavor** to your writing?

How can you help someone else **spice up** their writing?

LET'S COOK UP A TASTY BURGER!

Write a topic sentence that tells what the paragraph or story is mostly about. (Big idea—strong enough to hold lots of juicy details.)

First, add a *tasty topping* that gives one interesting detail that expands on the topic sentence. (Detail #1 sentence.)

Next, add a second topping that gives a tasty tidbit—more detail—and make sure it's intriguing. (Detail #2 sentence.)

Then, add a third topping—another delicious detail. (Detail #3 sentence.)

After that, add still another delicious detail. (Detail #4 sentence.)

Finally, write a concluding sentence that wraps it all up! (Aligns with the topic sentence to hold all the juicy details together!)

To order copies of this book direct from the publisher go to ParaklesisPressBooks.com. Discounts available for bulk orders; write to sales@ParaklesisPress.com for details.

Reviews help others find our books and buy our books. And they also help us know what kinds of books you want us to publish. So, if you liked this book and want to see more like it, please leave a review on Amazon, Goodreads, or wherever you buy and discuss books.

If you'd like to be entered to win books and merch, please sign up for a our monthly newsletter at ParaklesisPress.com/updates or use the handy, dandy QR code. We pick one winner each month from all our newsletter subscribers.

Thanks ever so much!